CARS, CARS, CARS

SMALL CARS

by Barbara Alpert

Gail Saunders-Smith, PhD, Consulting Editor

Consultant: Leslie Mark Kendall, Curator
Petersen Automotive Museum
Los Angeles, California

CAPSTONE PRESS
a capstone imprint

Pebble Plus is published by Capstone Press,
1710 Roe Crest Drive, North Mankato, Minnesota 56003.
www.capstonepub.com

Library of Congress Cataloging-in-Publication Data
Alpert, Barbara.
 Small cars / by Barbara Alpert.
   p. cm.—(Pebble plus. Cars, cars, cars)
 Summary: "Simple text and color photographs describe nine small cars"—Provided by the publisher.
 Audience: K-3.
 Includes bibliographical references and index.
 ISBN 978-1-62065-087-5 (library binding)
 ISBN 978-1-62065-879-6 (paperback)
 ISBN 978-1-4765-1077-4 (eBook PDF)
 1. Automobiles—Juvenile literature. 2. Compact cars—Juvenile literature. I. Title. II. Series: Pebble plus. Cars, cars, cars.
 TL147.A454 2013
 629.222—dc23   2012031834

Editorial Credits
Erika L. Shores, editor; Kyle Grenz, designer; Laura Manthe, production specialist

Photo Credits
Alamy: Steven May, 15; AP Images: Paul Sancya, 13, The Tennessean/Shelley Mays, 21; Getty Images: Jeff T. Green, 17; Shutterstock: 1xpert, cover (background), Max Earey, cover (right), 9; Wikimedia: Bull-Doser/public domain, cover (left), El Monty/CC BY-SA 3.0, 19, Mariordo/CC BY-SA 3.0, 7, Motohide Miwa/CC BY 2.0, 11, Ojp24/CC BY-SA 3.0, 5

Artistic Effects
Shutterstock: 1xpert

Note to Parents and Teachers

The Cars, Cars, Cars set supports national science standards related to science, technology, and society. This book describes and illustrates small cars. The images support early readers in understanding the text. The repetition of words and phrases helps early readers learn new words. This book also introduces early readers to subject-specific vocabulary words, which are defined in the Glossary section. Early readers may need assistance to read some words and to use the Table of Contents, Glossary, Read More, Internet Sites, and Index sections of the book.

Printed in the United States   5519

Table of Contents

Small

They're tiny! They're mini!
Small cars don't hold a lot,
but they're big energy savers.

Some Fiat 500s have
three doors and four seats.
Only kids or groceries fit
easily in the backseat.

Car length: 11.7 feet (3.6 meters)

A Think City car runs
on batteries instead of gas.
Plug it in for eight hours
and it will drive 100 miles
(161 kilometers).

Car length: 10.3 feet (3.14 meters)

The tiny Tata Pixel can turn
around in a tight circle.
The doors lift and lower
like the wings of a bird.

Car length: 10.2 feet (3.11 meters)

Smaller

The Scion iQ is made for
driving in crowded cities.
It parks in tight spaces
and steers easily between cars.

Car length: 10 feet (3 meters)

The Smart Fortwo may be small,

but you can't miss it on the streets.

Colorful paint jobs help

these cars stand out.

Car length: 8.8 feet (2.68 meters)

The electric Reva G-Wiz is made in India. Eight batteries under the front seats power this mini car.

Car length: 8.7 feet (2.65 meters)

Smallest

The Tango's body is half
as wide as a regular car's.
But the Tango is tough enough
to race. A powerful electric motor
hides near each back wheel.

Car length: 8.5 feet (2.6 meters)

The Lumeneo Smera has four wheels, but it drives like a motorcycle. This electric car tilts when it goes around curves.

Car length: 8.2 feet (2.5 meters)

The tiny three-wheeled Peel P50

has one headlight and one door.

Only the driver with a briefcase

or grocery bag can squeeze inside.

Car length: 4.5 feet (1.37 meters)

Glossary

battery—a container holding chemicals that store and create electricity

briefcase—a bag with a handle, used for carrying papers

crowded—very full, usually with many people

electric—having or using electricity

energy—the ability to do work, such as moving things or giving heat or light

headlight—a light in front of a car to show the road ahead

steer—to move in a certain direction

tilt—to lean to one side

Read More

Abramovitz, Melissa. *Silly Cars.* Cars, Cars, Cars. North Mankato, Minn.: Capstone Press, 2013.

Nixon, James. *Cars.* Machines on the Move. Mankato, Minn.: Amicus, 2011.

Von Finn, Denny. *Concept Cars.* Cool Rides. Minneapolis: Bellwether Media, 2010.

Internet Sites

FactHound offers a safe, fun way to find Internet sites related to this book. All of the sites on FactHound have been researched by our staff.

Here's all you do:

Visit *www.facthound.com*

Type in this code: 9781620650875

Check out projects, games and lots more at
www.capstonekids.com

23

Index

Word Count: 211
Grade: 1
Early-Intervention Level: 23